White House Wisdom:

A Book of Presidential Quotations

White House Wisdom:

A Book of
Presidential Quotations

Edited by William C. MacKay

BARNES
& NOBLE
BOOKS
NEW YORK

Compilation copyright © 2004 by Barnes & Noble, Inc.

2004 Barnes & Noble Books

ISBN 0-7607-4885-3

Printed and bound in the United States of America

04 05 06 07 08 09 HC 9 8 7 6 5 4 3 2 1

Study men, not historians.

—HARRY S. TRUMAN

Think of your forefathers! Think of your posterity.

—JOHN QUINCY ADAMS

Introduction

PRESIDENTS PAY A HIGH TOLL. "IN OUR BRIEF NATIONAL history," P. J. O'Rourke computed, "we have shot four of our presidents, worried five of them to death, impeached two and hounded another out of office. And when all else fails, we hold an election and assassinate their character."

And yet, we Americans revere our chief executives, often uncritically; sometimes against the best evidence. Other positions offer less stress, more lucrative benefits, or more uncontested glamour, but none can match the presidency's prestige. Henry Clay famously asserted that he would rather be right than be president, but historians recall that the Kentucky senator sought the White House no fewer than five times. "The office of the presidency," as Lyndon Johnson proudly asserted, "is the *only* office in this land of all the people."

The office of the presidency is also a bully pulpit; a podium for high principles and brass-tack politics; a statesman's perch and a scoundrel's refuge. The cumulative speeches and letters of our present and former chief executives constitute an *essence* of our history, a vibrant forum of all our differences and all that we hold most dear. I have gathered this anthology of presidential quotations as an echo chamber and an instigation; a humble attempt to reassert the worth of what our leaders have said.

As poet Marianne Moore noted, omissions are not accidents. It is no accident that readers will find herein no snippets of presidential gaffes or twisted locutions. The verbal mistakes or syntactical blunders of a commander in chief may or may not have relevance in a presidential campaign, but in this context, they would only distract, diminish and confuse.

One last, very personal note. I grew up in a household where newspaper reading and political debates were intense daily activities. My father always maintained, often to my disadvantage, that one should not take a position on an issue until he or she was capable of arguing both sides. In these divisive times, when discussion has dwindled into glittering generalities and sound-bite accusations, I remember that admonishment. It seems ever more imperative that we learn to listen again to history.

—W.C.M.

First, A Roll-Call of Presidents...

Liberty, when it begins to take root, is a plant of rapid growth.

—GEORGE WASHINGTON

Let every sluice of knowledge be open and set a-flowing

—JOHN ADAMS

That government is best which governs the least, because its people discipline themselves.

—THOMAS JEFFERSON

The problem to be solved is, not what form of government is perfect, but which of the forms is least imperfect.

—JAMES MADISON

The American continents...are henceforth not to be considered as subjects for future colonization by any European powers.

—JAMES MONROE

Always vote for principle, though you may vote alone, and you may cherish the sweetest reflection that your vote is never lost.

—JOHN QUINCY ADAMS

Our Federal Union: It must be preserved.

—ANDREW JACKSON

I make it a point never to write...the folk of Washington, unless I feel confidence that my doing so will lead to success.... I prefer to move step by step.

—Martin Van Buren

A decent and manly examination of the acts of government should not only be tolerated, but encouraged.

—William Henry Harrison

If the tide of defamation and abuse shall turn, and my administration come to be praised, future vice presidents who may succeed to the presidency may feel some slight encouragement to pursue an independent course.

—John Tyler

In truth, though I occupy a very high position, I am the hardest working man in this country.

—JAMES K. POLK

I informed [Alexander Stephens, a fellow Southern congressman] that if they were taken in rebellion against the Union, I would them with less reluctance than I had hung [sic] deserters and spies in Mexico!

—ZACHARY TAYLOR

In the North I was charged with being a pro-slavery man, seeking to extend slavery over free territory and in the South I was accused of being an abolitionist. But I am neither.

—MILLARD FILLMORE

I hate war in all its aspects. I deem it unworthy of the age in which I live.

—Franklin Pierce

What is right and what is practicable are two different things.

—James Buchanan

"A house divided against itself cannot stand." I believe the government cannot endure, permanently half slave and half free. I do not expect the Union to be dissolved—I do not expect the house to fall—but I *do* expect it will cease to be divided. It will become *all* one thing, or *all* the other.

—Abraham Lincoln

The times we live in are not without instruction. The American people must be taught—if they do not already feel—that treason is a crime and must be punished; that the government will not always bear with its enemies; that it is strong not only to protect but to punish.

—ANDREW JOHNSON

I did not want the Presidency, and I have never quite forgiven myself for resigning the command of the army to accept it.... War and politics are so different.

—ULYSSES S. GRANT

Coming in, I was denounced as a fraud by all the extreme men of the opposing party, and as an ingrate and a traitor by the same class of men in my own party. Going out, I have the good will, blessings, and approval of the best people of all parties.

—RUTHERFORD B. HAYES

A pound of pluck is worth a ton of luck.

—JAMES A. GARFIELD

I am an advocate of paper money, but that paper money must represent what it professes on its face. I do not wish to hold in my hands the printed lies of the government.

—CHESTER A. ARTHUR

Honor lies in honest toil.

—GROVER CLEVELAND

The manner by which women are treated is a good criterion to judge the true state of society. If we know but this one feature in a character of a nation, we may easily judge the rest, for as society advances, the true character of women is discovered.

—BENJAMIN HARRISON

I am no longer called the President of a party. I am now the President of the whole people.

—WILLIAM MCKINLEY,
after the Spanish-American War

There is a homely adage which runs, speak softly and carry a big stick; you will go far. If the American nation will speak softly and yet build and keep at a pitch of the highest training a thoroughly efficient navy, the Monroe Doctrine will go far.

—THEODORE ROOSEVELT

The world is not going to be saved by legislation.

—WILLIAM HOWARD TAFT

The world must be safe for democracy. Its peace must be planted upon trusted foundations of political liberty.

—WOODROW WILSON

America's present need is not heroic, but healing; not nostrums but normalcy; not revolution, but restoration.

—WARREN HARDING

The chief business of the American people is business.

—CALVIN COOLIDGE

The American system of rugged individualism.

—HERBERT HOOVER

I pledge you, I pledge myself to a new deal for the American people.

—Franklin Delano Roosevelt

It's a recession when you neighbor loses his job; it's a depression when you lose yours.

—Harry S. Truman

Every gun that is made, every warship launched, every rocket fired signifies, in the final sense, a theft from those who hunger and are not fed, those who are cold and are not clothed.

—Dwight D. Eisenhower

Let the word go forth from this time and place, to friend and foe alike, that the torch has been passed to a new generation of Americans, born in this century, tempered by war, disciplined by a hard and bitter peace, proud of our ancient heritage, and unwilling to witness or permit the slow undoing of those human rights to which this nation has always been committed, and to which we are committed today at home and around the world.

—JOHN F. KENNEDY

In your time we have the opportunity to move not only upward the rich society and the powerful society, but upward toward the Great Society.

—LYNDON B. JOHNSON

You can not win a battle in any arena merely by defending yourself.

—RICHARD M. NIXON

Our long national nightmare is over. Our Constitution works; our great Republic is a government of laws and not men.

—GERALD FORD

America did not invent human rights. In a very real sense, human rights invented America.

—JIMMY CARTER

Mr. Gorbachev, tear down this wall!

—RONALD REAGAN

I want a kinder, gentler nation.

—GEORGE H. W. BUSH

There is nothing wrong with America that cannot be cured with what is right in America.

—BILL CLINTON

Terrorist attacks can shake the foundations of our biggest buildings, but they cannot touch the foundation of America. These acts shatter steel, but they cannot dent the steel of American resolve.

—GEORGE W. BUSH

Presidential
Wisdom

My movements to the chair of government will be accompanied by feelings not unlike those of a culprit who is going to the place of execution; so unwilling am I, in the evening of a life nearly consumed in public cares, to quit a peaceful abode for an ocean of difficulties, without that competency of political skills, abilities and inclination which is necessary to manage the helm.

—GEORGE WASHINGTON, before departing Mt. Vernon
to become president

If you are as happy, my dear sir, on entering this house as I am leaving it and returning home, [then] you are the happiest man in the country.

—JAMES BUCHANAN, to his successor
Abraham Lincoln

No other President ever enjoyed the Presidency as I did!

—THEODORE ROOSEVELT

The president is like a jackass standing alone in the middle of a field in a driving hailstorm. There's nothing he can do but stand there and take it.

—LYNDON JOHNSON, to his successor
Richard Nixon

When we got into office, the first thing that surprised me most was to find that things were just as bad as we'd been saying they were.

—JOHN F. KENNEDY

The idea that I should become President seems to me too visionary to require a serious answer. It has never entered my head, nor is it likely to enter the head of any other person.

—ZACHARY TAYLOR

I know what I am fit for. I can command a body of men in a rough way; but I am not fit to be President.

—ANDREW JACKSON

I am a man of reserved, cold, austere and forbidding manners; my political adversaries say, a gloomy misanthropist and my personal enemies, an unsocial savage.

—JOHN QUINCY ADAMS

I have never been in doubt since I was old enough to think intelligently that I would someday be made president.

—WILLIAM MCKINLEY

I never really had any affinity for politics. I've always looked on politics as a means to an end… It has never been a natural part of my life.

—JIMMY CARTER

Any man who wants to be president is either an egomaniac or crazy.

—DWIGHT D. EISENHOWER

No man who ever held the office of President would congratulate a friend on obtaining it. He will make one man ungrateful, and a hundred men his enemies, for every office he can bestow.

—JOHN ADAMS

I have come to the conclusion that the major part of the work a President is to increase the gate receipts of expositions and fairs and bring tourists into town.

—WILLIAM HOWARD TAFT

The opportunist thinks of me and today. The statesman thinks of us and tomorrow.

—DWIGHT D. EISENHOWER

A politician is a man who understands government. A statesman is a politician who's been dead ten or fifteen years.

—HARRY S. TRUMAN

The one thing sure about politics is that what goes up comes down and what goes down often comes up.

—RICHARD M. NIXON

I cannot tell a lie.

—GEORGE WASHINGTON, apocryphal

Truth is the glue that holds government together.

—GERALD FORD

There can be no whitewash at the White House.

—RICHARD M. NIXON

If it were not for the reporters I would tell the truth.

—CHESTER A. ARTHUR

If one morning I walked on top of the water across the Potomac, the headline that morning would read *President Can't Swim!*

—LYNDON JOHNSON

I would honor the man who would give to his country a good newspaper.

—RUTHERFORD B. HAYES

The man who reads nothing at all is better educated than the man who reads nothing but newspapers.

—THOMAS JEFFERSON

The men with the muck-rakes are often indispensable to the wellbeing of society; but only if they know when to stop raking the mud.

—THEODORE ROOSEVELT

Before I refuse to take your questions, I have an opening statement.

—RONALD REAGAN

Were it left to me to decide whether we should have a government without newspapers or newspapers without government, I should not hesitate a moment to prefer the latter.

—THOMAS JEFFERSON

Information is the oxygen of the modern age. It seeps through the walls topped by barbed wire, it wafts across the electrified borders.

—RONALD REAGAN

Liberty is to faction what air is to fire, an ailment without which it instantly expires. But it could not be less folly to abolish liberty, which is essential to political life, because it nourishes faction than it would be to wish the annihilation of air, which is essential to animal life, because it imparts to fire its destructive agency.

—JAMES MADISON

I have never been hurt by anything I didn't say.

—CALVIN COOLIDGE

The White House is a bully pulpit.

—THEODORE ROOSEVELT

You have summoned me in my weakness. You must sustain me in your strength.

—FRANKLIN PIERCE

It is a condition which confronts us—not a theory.

—GROVER CLEVELAND

What we believe in is what works.

—BILL CLINTON

Abstract propositions should never be discussed by a legislative body.

—JAMES BUCHANAN

I played by the rules of politics as I found them.

—Richard M. Nixon

All free governments are managed by the combined wisdom and folly of the people.

—James A. Garfield

A government that remembers that the people are its master is a good and needed thing.

—George H.W. Bush

Men may die, but the fabrics of free institutions remain unshaken.

—Chester A. Arthur

Those who deny freedom to others, deserve it not for themselves; and, under a just God, can not long retain it.

—ABRAHAM LINCOLN

Liberty cannot be preserved without a general knowledge among the people.

—JOHN ADAMS

A president does not shape a new and personal vision of American. He collects it from the scattered hopes of the American past.

—LYNDON B. JOHNSON

Minds do not act together in public; they simply stick together; and when their private activities are resumed, they fly apart again.

—GROVER CLEVELAND

The real political issues of the day declare themselves, and come out of the depths of that deep which we call public opinion.

—JAMES A. GARFIELD

Great innovations should not be forced on slender majorities.

—THOMAS JEFFERSON

One man with courage makes a majority

—ANDREW JACKSON

[The President is] the last person in the world to know what the people really want and think.

—JAMES A. GARFIELD

If you fear making anyone mad, then you ultimately probe for the lowest common denominator of human achievement

—JIMMY CARTER

Popularity, I have always thought, may aptly be compared to a coquette: the more you woo her, the more apt is she to elude your embrace.

—JOHN TYLER

I sit here all day trying to persuade people to do the things they ought to have sense enough to do without my persuading them.... That's all the powers of the president amount to.

—HARRY S. TRUMAN

There is one thing about being president: Nobody can tell you when to sit down.

—DWIGHT D. EISENHOWER

A good leader can not get too far ahead of his followers.

—FRANKLIN DELANO ROOSEVELT

Politics is a war of causes; a joust of principles.

—WOODROW WILSON

Our differences are politics. Our agreements are principles

—WILLIAM MCKINLEY

I wish to preach, not the doctrine of ignoble ease, but the doctrine of the strenuous life.

—THEODORE ROOSEVELT

A people that values its privileges above its principles soon loses both.

—DWIGHT D. EISENHOWER

In politics, the middle way is none at all.

—JAMES A. GARFIELD

If you can't stand the heat, get out of the kitchen.

—HARRY S. TRUMAN

Presidents in the past have always been better than their adversaries have predicted.

—RUTHERFORD B. HAYES

No man will ever bring out of the presidency the reputation which carries him into it.

—THOMAS JEFFERSON

You have heard the story, haven't you, about the man who was tarred and feathered and carried out of town on a rail? A man in the crowd asked him how he liked it. His reply was that if it was not for the honor of the thing, he would much rather walk.

—ABRAHAM LINCOLN

The best executive is the one who has sense enough to pick good men to do what he wants done, and self-restraint enough to keep from meddling with them while they do it.

—THEODORE ROOSEVELT

In preparing for battle I have always found that plans are useless, but planning is indispensable.

—DWIGHT D. EISENHOWER

Fighting battles is like courting girls: those who make the most pretensions and are boldest usually win.

—RUTHERFORD B. HAYES

Finishing second in the Olympics gets you silver. Finishing second in politics gets you oblivion.

—RICHARD M. NIXON

Washington is a very easy city for you to forget where you came from and why you got there in the first place.

—HARRY S. TRUMAN

There are a number of things wrong with Washington. One of them is that everyone has been too long away from home.

—Dwight D. Eisenhower

You know what's interesting about Washington? It's the kind of place where second-guessing has become second nature.

—George W. Bush

I have no trouble with my enemies. I can take care of my enemies in a fight. But my friends, my god-damned friends, they're the ones who keep me walking the floor at nights.

—Warren G. Harding

My country has in its wisdom contrived for me the most insignificant office [the vice presidency] that ever the invention of man contrived or his imagination conceived; and as I can do neither good nor evil, I must be borne away by others and meet the common fate.

—JOHN ADAMS

A man who has never lost himself in a cause bigger than himself has missed one of life's mountain-top experiences. Only in losing himself does he find himself.

—RICHARD NIXON

For this is what America is all about. It is the uncrossed desert and the unclimbed ridge. It is the star that is not reached and the harvest that is sleeping in the unplowed ground

—LYNDON B. JOHNSON

I would rather believe something and suffer for it, than to slide along into success without opinions.

—JAMES A. GARFIELD

It is a great advantage to a President and a major source of safety to the country, for him to know that he is not a great man.

—CALVIN COOLIDGE

To those of you who received honors, awards and distinctions, I say well done. And to the "C" students, I say: You, too, can be president of the United States.

—GEORGE W. BUSH, speaking at a Yale University graduation

When you get to be President, there are all those things, the honors, the twenty-one gun salutes, all those things. You have to remember it isn't for you. It's for the Presidency.

—HARRY S. TRUMAN

Every man who takes office in Washington either grows or swells, and when I give a man office I watch him carefully to see whether is growing or swelling.

—WOODROW WILSON

A little flattery will support a man through great fatigue.

—JAMES MONROE

A public man must never forget that he loses his usefulness when he as an individual, rather than his policy, becomes the issue.

—RICHARD M. NIXON

One cool judgment is worth a thousand hasty councils.

—WOODROW WILSON

Actions speak louder than words.

—THEODORE ROOSEVELT

The most valuable of all talents is that of never using two words when one will do.

—THOMAS JEFFERSON

Abuse of words has been the great instrument of sophistry and chicanery, of party, faction, and division of society.

—JOHN ADAMS

That depends on what your definition of "is" is.

—BILL CLINTON

We cannot learn from one another until we stop shouting at each other; until we speak quietly enough so that our words can be heard as well as our voices.

—RICHARD M. NIXON

You ain't learnin' nothin' when you're talkin'.

—LYNDON B. JOHNSON

No terms except unconditional and immediate surrender can be accepted.

ULYSSES S. GRANT, 1862

The war is over—the rebels are our countrymen again.

—ULYSSES S. GRANT, 1865

It would be judicious to act with magnanimity towards a prostrate foe.

—ZACHARY TAYLOR, 1846

Tell him to go to hell.

> —ZACHARY TAYLOR, on Santa Ana's demand
> for surrender, 1847

I am as fit as a bull moose and you can use me to the limit.

> —THEODORE ROOSEVELT

Please tell me that you're Republicans.

> —RONALD REAGAN, to surgeons about to operate on
> him after assassination attempt

It was involuntary. They sunk my boat.

> —JOHN F. KENNEDY, on being a war hero

Fear is the foundation of most governments.

—John Adams

We have nothing to fear but fear itself—nameless, unreasoning, unjustified terror which paralyzes needed effort to convert retreat into advance.

—Franklin Delano Roosevelt

Since the general civilization of mankind, I believe there are more instances of the abridgement of the freedom of the people by gradual and silent encroachments of those in power than by violent and sudden usurpations.

—James Madison

I welcome this kind of examination because people have got to know whether or not their President is a crook. Well, I'm not a crook.

—Richard M. Nixon

I am a Ford, not a Lincoln.

—Gerald Ford

I may be president of the United States, but my private life is nobody's damned business!

—Chester A. Arthur

I did not have sexual relations with that woman, Miss Lewinsky.

—Bill Clinton

I do not think it altogether inappropriate to introduce myself to this audience. I am the man who accompanied Jacqueline Kennedy to Paris and I have enjoyed it.

—JOHN F. KENNEDY

There is nothing stable but Heaven and the Constitution.

—JAMES BUCHANAN

And lastly, let us provide in our constitution for its revision at stated periods.

—THOMAS JEFFERSON

Don't interfere with anything in the Constitution. That must be maintained, for it is the only safeguard to our liberties.

—ABRAHAM LINCOLN

Each public officer who takes an oath to support the constitution swears that he will support it as he understands it, and not as it is understood by others.

—ANDREW JACKSON

The storm of frenzy and faction must inevitably dash itself in vain against the unshaken rock of the Constitution.

—FRANKLIN PIERCE

America has never been united by blood or birth or soil. We are bound by ideals that move us beyond our backgrounds, lift us above our interests and teach us what it means to be citizens.

—GEORGE W. BUSH

In a body [like Congress] where there are more than one hundred talking lawyers, you can make no calculation upon the termination of any debate.

—FRANKLIN PIERCE

I like the noise of democracy.

—JAMES BUCHANAN

I have always been among those who believed that the greatest freedom of speech was the greatest safety, because if a man is a fool, the best thing to do is to encourage him to advertise the fact by speaking.

—WOODROW WILSON

Throughout history, attempts to micromanage casual conversation have only incited distrust. They have invited people to look for an insult in every word; gesture; action. And in their own Orwellian way, crusades that demand correct behavior crush diversity in the name of diversity

—GEORGE H.W. BUSH

If we cannot end now our difference, at least we can help make the world safe for diversity.

—JOHN F. KENNEDY

We become not a melting pot but a beautiful mosaic. Different people, different beliefs, different yearnings, different hopes, different dreams.

—JIMMY CARTER

It has been said that politics is the second oldest profession. I have learned that it bears a striking resemblance to the first.

—RONALD REAGAN

When I came into power, I found that the party managers had taken it all to themselves. I could not name my own cabinet. They sold out every place to pay the election expense.

—BENJAMIN HARRISON

A man who will steal *for* me will steal *from* me.

THEODORE ROOSEVELT, explaining a firing

A republic without parties is a complete anomaly. The history of all popular governments show how absurd is the idea of their attempting to exist without parties.

—FRANKLIN PIERCE

There is more selfishness and less principle among members of Congress...than I had any conception of, before I became President of the U.S.

—JAMES POLK

Though total agreement between the Executive and the Congress is impossible, total respect is important.

—LYNDON B. JOHNSON

When they call the roll in the Senate, the Senators do not know whether to answer "Present" or "Not Guilty."

—THEODORE ROOSEVELT

My choice early in life was either to be a piano player in a whorehouse or a politician; and, to tell the truth, there's hardly a difference.

—HARRY S. TRUMAN

The people are responsible for the character of their Congress. If that body be ignorant, reckless, and corrupt, it is because the people tolerate ignorance, recklessness, and corruption. If it be intelligent, brave, and pure, it is because the people demand these high qualities to represent them in the national legislature.

—JAMES A. GARFIELD

The purpose of foreign policy is not to provide an outlet for our own sentiments or hope or indignation; it is to shape real events in a real world.

—JOHN F. KENNEDY

Peace, commerce, and honest friendship, with all nations—entangling alliances with none.

—THOMAS JEFFERSON

America cannot be an ostrich with its head in the sand.

—WOODROW WILSON

Our idea is to create a situation which those lands to which we have obligations or in which we have interests, if they are ready to fight a fire, should be able to count on us to furnish the hose and water.

—RICHARD M. NIXON

We Americans have no commission from God to police the world.

—BENJAMIN HARRISON

The United States is not a nation to which peace is a necessity.

—GROVER CLEVELAND

To be prepared for war is one of the most effectual means of preserving peace.

—GEORGE WASHINGTON

The American people are slow to wrath, but when their wrath is once kindled it burns like a consuming flame

—THEODORE ROOSEVELT

For mere revenge I would do nothing. This nation is too great to look for mere revenge. But for the security of the future I would do everything.

—JAMES A. GARFIELD

War should never be entered upon until every agency of peace has failed.

—William McKinley

Patriotism means to stand by the country. It does not mean to stand by the president.

—Theodore Roosevelt

Our forbearance should never be misunderstood. Our reluctance for conflict should not be misjudged as a failure of will. When action is required to preserve our national security, we will act.

—Ronald Reagan

Of all the enemies to liberty, war is, perhaps, the most to be dreaded, because it comprises and develops the germ of every other. In war, the discretionary power of the Executive is extended; its influence in dealing out offices, honors, and emoluments is multiplied; and all the means of seducing the minds, are added to those of subduing the force, of the people. War, is in fact the true nurse of executive aggrandizement.

—JAMES MADISON

Of the four wars in my lifetime, none came about because the U.S. was too strong.

—RONALD REAGAN

Isolationism is the road to war. Worse than that, isolationism is the road to defeat in war.

—HARRY S. TRUMAN

There's an old saying that victory has a hundred fathers, but defeat is an orphan.

—JOHN F. KENNEDY

No nation can preserve its freedom in the midst of continual warfare.

—JAMES MADISON

This administration today, here and now, declares unconditional war on poverty.

—LYNDON B. JOHNSON

I have never advocated war except as a means of peace.

—Ulysses S. Grant

There can be no law if we were to invoke one code of international conduct for those who oppose us and another for our friends.

—Dwight D. Eisenhower

I would rather have peace than be president.

—Harry S. Truman

Books can not be killed by fire. People die, but books never die. No man and no force can abolish memory.

—Franklin Delano Roosevelt

I destroy my enemies when I make them my friends.

—ABRAHAM LINCOLN

Government is not reason; it is not eloquence; it is force. Like fire, it is a dangerous servant and a fearful master.

—GEORGE WASHINGTON

The history of liberty is a history of resistance. The history of liberty is a history of the limitation of governmental power, not the increase of it.

—WOODROW WILSON

If tyranny and oppression come to this land, it will be in the guise of fighting a foreign enemy.

—JAMES MADISON

What do you mean by the Revolution? The war? That was no part of the revolution; it was only an effect and consequence of it. The resolution was in the minds of the people, and this was effected from 1760 to 1775, in the course of fifteen years, before a drop of blood was shot at Lexington.

—JOHN ADAMS

Those who make peaceful revolution impossible will make violent revolution inevitable.

—JOHN F. KENNEDY

The price of freedom is eternal vigilance.

—GEORGE WASHINGTON

Fourscore and seven years ago our fathers brought forth upon this continent a new nation, conceived in liberty, and dedicated to the proposition that all men are created equal.

—ABRAHAM LINCOLN

Lives of nations are determined not by the count of years, but by the lifetime of the human spirit. The life of a man is threescore and ten; a little more, a little less. The life of a nation is the fullness of the measure of its will to live.

—FRANKLIN DELANO ROOSEVELT

Freedom is a fragile thing and is never more than one generation away from extinction. It is not ours by inheritance; it must be fought for and defended constantly by each generation, for it comes only once to a people. Those who have known freedom, and then lost it, have never known it again.

—RONALD REAGAN

I contend that the strongest of all governments is that which is most free.

—WILLIAM HENRY HARRISON

It is not our frowning battlement…or the strength of our gallant and disciplined army…. Our defense is in the preservation of the spirit which prizes liberty as the heritage of all men, in all lands, everywhere.

—ABRAHAM LINCOLN

The dangers of a concentration of all power in the general government of a confederacy so vast as ours are too obvious to be disregarded.

—Franklin Pierce

And so, my fellow Americans, ask not what your country can do for you—ask what you can do for your country.

—John F. Kennedy

I hold it, that a little rebellion, now and then, is a good thing, and as necessary in the political world as storms in the physical.

—Thomas Jefferson

The people, when they have been unchecked, have been as unjust, tyrannical, brutal, barbarous, and cruel as an king or senate possessed of uncontrollable power. The majority has eternally, and without exception, usurped over the rights of the minority.

—JOHN ADAMS

I'm convinced more than ever that man finds liberation only when he binds himself to God and commits himself to his fellow man.

—RONALD REAGAN

I know that Lord is always on the side of the right. But it is my constant anxiety and prayer that I and this nation should be on the Lord's side.

—ABRAHAM LINCOLN

The Presidency brings no special gift of prophecy or foresight. You take an oath, you step into an office, and you must then help guide a great democracy.

—LYNDON B. JOHNSON

Faith...teaches us not merely to tolerate one another, but to respect one another—to show a regard for different views and the courtesy to listen. This is essential to democracy.

—GEORGE W. BUSH

All forms of religion have united for the first time to diffuse charity and piety, because for the first time in the history of nations all have been totally untrammeled and absolutely free.

—MARTIN VAN BUREN

That to compel a man to furnish contributions of money for the propagation of opinions which he disbelieves and abhors, is sinful and tyrannical.

—THOMAS JEFFERSON

In the emerging global economy, everything is mobile: capital, factories; even entire industries. The only resource that is really rooted in a nation—and the ultimate source of all its wealth—is its people.

—BILL CLINTON

If you want to make enemies, try to change something.

—WOODROW WILSON

It is not strange...to mistake change for progress.

—MILLARD FILLMORE

When you see ten troubles rolling down the road, if you don't do anything, nine of them will roll into a ditch before they get to you.

—CALVIN COOLIDGE

While all other sciences have advanced, that of government is at a standstill—little better understood, little better practiced now than three or four thousand years ago.

—JOHN ADAMS

One thing is sure. We have to do something. We have to do the best we know how at the moment. If it doesn't turn out right, we can modify it as we go along.

—Franklin Delano Roosevelt

There has been something crude and heartless and unfeeling in our haste to succeed and be great. Our thought has been 'Let every man look out for himself, let every generation look out for itself,' while we reared giant machinery which made it impossible that any but those who stood at the levers of control should have a chance to look out for themselves.

—Woodrow Wilson

The purpose of politics is to give people tools to make the most of their lives

—Bill Clinton

All the measures of the government are directed to the purpose of making the rich richer and the poor poorer.

—WILLIAM HENRY HARRISON

If a free society cannot help the many who are poor; it cannot save the few who are rich.

—JOHN F. KENNEDY

And government, like any family, can for a year spend a little more than it earns. But you and I know that a continuation of that habit means the poorhouse.

—FRANKLIN DELANO ROOSEVELT

As an individual who undertakes to live by borrowing, soon finds his original means devoured by interest, and next no one left to borrow from; so must it be with a government.

—ABRAHAM LINCOLN

The deficit is big enough to take care of itself.

—RONALD REAGAN

Blessed are the young, for they shall inherit the national debt.

—HERBERT HOOVER

You can not stop the spread of an idea by passing a law against it.

—HARRY S. TRUMAN

I know no method to secure the repeal of bad or obnoxious laws so effective as their stringent execution.

—Ulysses S. Grant

It is much more important to kill bad bills than to pass good ones.

—Calvin Coolidge

No man has ever yet been hanged for breaking the spirit of a law.

—Grover Cleveland

There is nothing new in the world except the history you do not know.

—Harry S. Truman

Trust the people: that is the crucial lesson of history.

—RONALD REAGAN

History, in general, only informs us what bad government is.

—THOMAS JEFFERSON

The past sharpens perspective, warns of pitfalls, and helps to point the way.

—DWIGHT D. EISENHOWER

History teaches perhaps few lessons. But surely one such lesson learned by the world at great cost is that aggression unopposed becomes a dangerous disease.

—JIMMY CARTER

Recognizing and confronting our history is important. Transcending our history is essential. We are not limited by what we have done, or what we have left undone. We are limited only by what we are willing to do.

—George W. Bush

Once you get into this great stream of history you can't get out. You can drown or you can be pulled ashore by the tide.

—Richard M. Nixon

I claim not to have controlled events, but confess plainly that events have controlled me.

—Abraham Lincoln

A President does not shape a new and personal vision of America. He collects it from the scattered hopes of the American past.

—LYNDON B. JOHNSON

There's nothing better for the inside of a man than the outside of a horse.

—RONALD REAGAN

There are three things which are real: God, human folly and laughter. The first two are beyond our comprehension, so we must do what we can with the third.

—JOHN F. KENNEDY

The art of making love, muffled up in furs, in the open air, with the thermometer at zero, is a Yankee invention, which requires a Yankee poet, to describe.

—JOHN QUINCY ADAMS

If all that Americans want is security, they can go to prison. They'll have enough to eat, a bed and a roof over their heads. But if an American wants to preserve his dignity and his equality as a human being, he must not bow his neck to any dictatorial government.

—DWIGHT D. EISENHOWER

If a government is big enough to give you everything you want, it is big enough to take away everything you have.

—GERALD FORD

Just because we cannot do everything for everyone does not mean we should do nothing for anyone.

—BILL CLINTON

No government ever voluntarily reduces itself in size.

—RONALD REAGAN

To encourage literature and the arts is a duty which every good citizen owes to his country.

—GEORGE WASHINGTON

I must study politics and war that my sons may have liberty to study mathematics and philosophy. My sons ought to study mathematics and philosophy, geography, natural history, naval architecture, navigation, commerce and agriculture in order to give their children a right to study painting, poetry, music, architecture, statuary, tapestry, and porcelain.

—JOHN ADAMS

The human animal cannot be trusted for anything good except *en masse*. The combined thought and action of the whole people of any race, creed or nationality will always point in the right direction.

—HARRY S. TRUMAN

It has been my experience that folks who have no vices have very few virtues.

—ABRAHAM LINCOLN

A man who has never gone to school may steal from a freight car, but if he has a university education, he may steal the whole railroad.

—THEODORE ROOSEVELT

The free school is the promoter of that intelligence which is to preserve us as a nation. If we were to have another contest in the near future of our national existence, I predict that the dividing line will not be Mason's and Dixon's, but between patriotism and intelligence on one side, and superstition, ambition and ignorance on the other.

—ULYSSES S. GRANT

There are two types of education... One should teach us how to make a living, And the other how to live.

—JOHN ADAMS

If anyone tells you that America's best days are behind her, they're looking the wrong way.

—GEORGE H.W. BUSH

Politics is just like show business. You have a hell of an opening, coast for a while, and then have a hell of a close.

—RONALD REAGAN

I have not permitted myself, gentlemen, to con-
clude that I am the best man in the country; but
I am reminded, in this connection, of a story of an
old Dutch farmer who remarked to a companion
once that 'it was not best to swap horses while
crossing streams.'

—ABRAHAM LINCOLN

What is the use of being elected or reelected
unless you stand for something?

—GROVER CLEVELAND

If you think too much about being reelected, it is
very difficult to be worth reelecting.

—WOODROW WILSON

Old minds are like old horses; you must exercise them if you wish to keep them in working order.

—JOHN ADAMS

Well, there doesn't seem to be anything else for an ex-president to do but go into the country and raise big pumpkins.

—CHESTER A. ARTHUR

There is nothing in life so pathetic as a former president.

—JOHN QUINCY ADAMS

When our memories outweigh our dreams, we have grown old.

—BILL CLINTON

And still the question, "What shall be done with our ex-presidents?" is not laid at rest; and I sometimes think Watterson's solution of it, "Take them out and shoot them," is worthy of attention.

—GROVER CLEVELAND

Oh, that lovely title, ex-president.

—DWIGHT D. EISENHOWER

THE BUCK STOPS HERE.

—SIGN ON HARRY TRUMAN'S OVAL OFFICE DESK